MORNING STARS

OR,

NAMES OF CHRIST
FOR HIS LITTLE ONES

FRANCES RIDLEY HAVERGAL

SOLID GROUND CHRISTIAN BOOKS
BIRMINGHAM, ALABAMA USA

Solid Ground Christian Books
PO Box 660132
Vestavia Hills AL 35266
205-443-0311
sgcb@charter.net
www.solid-ground-books.com

MORNING STARS
Names of Christ for His Little Ones

Frances Ridley Havergal (1836-1879)

Taken from the 1881 edition by James Nisbet & Co., London

Cover design by Borgo Design
Contact them at borgogirl@bellsouth.net

ISBN- 978-159925-188-2

CONTENTS.

PREFATORY NOTE.

JUST a week before my dear sister F. R. H. died, I took her letters upstairs. Her pretty kittens Trot and Dot were playing on her bed. She was too ill to care about her letters, but was so pleased to get the first page of *this* book. She looked at it carefully, and with her pencil corrected mistakes. Then she was anxious every reader should have space to add the verses, and asked me to write about it. May I say that she hoped you would read one chapter daily! My dear sister intended writing another book for you, "Evening Stars; or, Promises for the Little Ones." But, though she is gone, the Promises are left. Will you not search them out in your Bibles every evening, and just say, as she often did, "This promise is so bright, and it is for me."

MARIA V. G. HAVERGAL.

September, 1879.

PREFACE.

To the Readers of "LITTLE PILLOWS,"
"MORNING BELLS," *and* "BRUEY."

WRITING to you does not seem
the least like writing an ordi-
nary "preface," all stiff and proper;
for so many of you have written to ask
me to write you another book, and so
many loving messages have reached
me from others, that we seem to be
"friends," don't we? So this comes
to you at last, with my love, and many
a prayer that it may lead you to look
oftener and more steadily at Jesus, the
Bright and Morning Star.

One thing I want you very much to
be quite clear about. No amount of
"good little books" will do you any
good unless they lead you to love the

Book of books. If you really love
Jesus you are quite sure to love His
word. But one reason why some of
you do not love it half as much as you
wish you did, is because you do not
know enough of it, and you only *read*,
you don't " *search* "; which is what God
expressly tells you to do. A capital
piece of advice was given by a man
who did a very great deal towards
leading people to love and know their
Bibles. He said : " When you take
your Bibles, you should be always
hunting for something ! " So I have
given you something to hunt for every
day. You will see that nearly every
time I have quoted a text I only tell
the chapter where it is to be found,
and leave a little blank space for the
verse. Now, not one of you is to
consider your copy of the book com-
plete till you have found out all these
verses and put them in yourself with
a nice fine pen or sharp pencil ! So,
you see, I have left *you* to finish the

book, and thus given you each "something to do" and something to hunt for, which I hope will be only a beginning of your hunting for a great deal more. Every verse that you find I should like you *also* to mark in your own Bibles; then you will find them again much more easily, and be often reminded of them in time to come.

Though you will find here thirty-one names of the Lord Jesus Christ, you must not think these are nearly all. Some I had written about before, such as "My King," "Our Surety," and others; and the rest had to be left out for want of room. But this is something else to be hunted for. Find out all the rest, and write them at the end of this book. And then, not till then, you may write "*Finis*"!

FRANCES RIDLEY HAVERGAL.

MORNING STARS.

Our Saviour.

"The Father sent the Son to be the Saviour of the world."—I JOHN iv.

WE must begin with this. For until we know the Lord Jesus as our Saviour, we cannot really know Him as anything else.

If you were drowning, it would be no use to call out to you about a kind friend who was ready to do all sorts of things for you. The first thing he would do for you would be to jump in and save you. So Jesus must be your Saviour first, and then all His other names will be precious and beautiful to you.

Perhaps you have heard the Lord Jesus spoken of as Friend, or Shepherd, or Master, and have thought how nice it would be if you could call Him so for yourself. And may be you wondered why the names which made others so glad did not seem to bring any gladness to you. This is because you had not begun at the beginning. And the beginning is the great fact that we are sinners, and cannot do without a Saviour. It does not matter how old or how young anybody is, God says " *all* have sinned," and " there is no difference." (Rom. iii. .) Not a bit of difference in His sight between you and a poor little untaught gutter child! Both are real sinners, and cannot be saved without a real Saviour; and Jesus is ready to save him and to save you, both alike. Some people will tell you you are better than they, because you have been brought up as a little Christian. But St. Paul himself said : "What then? Are we better than they? No; in no wise." (Rom. iii.   .) And surely, if St. Paul wanted a Saviour, you and I must want one. Jesus says He did not come to call the righteous (Matt. ix.   ); but He says, "The Son of Man is come to seek and to save that which was lost" (Luke xix.   ); and "Christ Jesus came into the world to save sinners" (1 Tim. i.   ).

So you see, Jesus did not come to have anything to do with us unless we own to being "lost" and "sinners." But if you say, "Yes, I am a sinner, and I am like the prodigal son, lost, and far away," then you are just the one that Jesus came to save. And then you may say, "Lord, save me" (Matt. xiv.   ); because you know you want saving. And then Jesus saves you surely and certainly, else He would not be a Saviour; for He is a Saviour because He saves, and this is what His very name means. (Matt. i. .) He is "a Saviour, and a great one" (Isa. xix.). He is "mighty to save" (Isa. lxiii.). And as soon as you come to Him for the salvation you want, you will say, "The Lord was ready to save *Me*." (Isa. xxxviii. .)

I must give you some verses written by a little girl named Alice, only eleven years old. You will see how she came to Jesus as her Saviour, and found this precious name true for herself. Come! and you will find it true for you, for He is "Jesus Christ, the *same* yesterday, and to-day, and for ever." (Heb. xiii. .)

One day I was in trouble,
    And my heart was sore distressed;
But Jesus came to me and said,
    "Come, and I will give you rest."

I went to Him, and told Him
    I'd a debt I could not pay;
He said to me, "Dost thou not know
    My blood washed it away?"

He took and laid me in His arms,
    With my head upon His breast,
And now I'm with my Saviour,
    I'm quiet and at rest.

I pray each day and every night,
    Dear friends, that all of you
May trust the loving Saviour,
    And be made happy too.

The Bright and Morning Star.

"I am . . . the Bright and Morning Star."
REV. xxii.

THIS name of the Lord Jesus seems as if it must be meant especially for children ; for it is those who get up early who see the beautiful morning star, shining in the quiet sky that is just beginning to be touched with a promise of dawn, and He says, " they that seek Me early shall find Me" (Prov. viii.   ).   A star shines out in the dark sky, and the darkness cannot put it out, but only makes it all the brighter.   So if we look up to Jesus as our Star, even if there seems nothing else to make us happy, and nothing to be seen but some dark trouble all around, He will shine in our hearts (2 Cor. iv.   ) ; and we shall have light and gladness in them. (Ps. iv. .)

A star is always true. If we were going in a wrong direction across a wide moor, directly we caught sight of a star that we knew, we should be shown our mistake. So when we think of Jesus we shall see whether we are going right or wrong, whether we are following Him or going away from Him. When we stop and say to ourselves, "what would Jesus do?" it is like looking up at the star to see which way to go.

Jesus calls Himself the Bright Star, for He is the Brightness of the Father's glory. (Heb. i.   .) Nothing makes any one look so bright as looking at His brightness and beauty. You could not possibly have a dismal face while you are really "looking unto Jesus" (Heb. xii.   ), any more than a little mirror would look dark if you held it up to catch the rays of a bright light.

He calls Himself the Morning Star too, because when we see that shining clear and still we know that the darkness is passing, and very soon the day will break and the shadows flee away. (Cant. ii.   .) The sight of the morning star is the promise of the day. And so if you get a little glimpse by faith of the brightness of the Lord Jesus Christ now, it is only a beginning of clearer sight, and a pledge of the glorious day that has no night, in the land where you shall see the King in His beauty.   (Isa. xxxiii.   .)

ᛋᚢᚱ ᚠᚱᛁᛖᚾᛞ.

Our Friend.

"This is my Friend."—CANT. v.

ONLY think of this! Think of the Lord Jesus Himself, whom all the angels of God worship (Heb. i.   ), the King of kings, full of glory and beauty, letting you look up to Him and say, " This is my Friend ! " May you really? Yes, *really*; for Jesus says, " I have called you friends." (John xv.   .)

It is so nice to have a real friend. Don't you feel as if you would do any-thing for your particular friend ? Don't you look forward to being together and telling each other everything ? Does it not make it a delightful day if your friend is coming ? But " what a Friend we have in Jesus!" A much more real friend than any one else! He loves you a great deal more, and thinks a great deal more about you, than the very dearest friend you ever had. He does not come just now and then, and leave you alone between whiles; but He is like a friend that always stays with us, so that any minute we may talk to Him and be happy with Him. Never any "good bye" in this wonderful friendship! (Heb. xiii.   .)

He is such a patient Friend. How very often we grieve Him, and do or say something that we know He would not like, and forget that He is there all the time! (Matt. xxviii.   .) And still He is our Friend, and forgives us, and goes on loving us.

He is such a kind Friend. Has He not been kind to you, now? Just think what you would do if He had not given you all the little mercies as well as the great ones around you ! (Isa. lxiii. .) See how He thinks of everything for you, so that they are new every morning. (Lam. iii. .)

He is such a wise Friend. He never makes a mistake in anything He sends you or bids you do ; even if you do not see at all why He lets something come that you do not like, you may be quite sure He is quite right.

He must be the most loving Friend, because He died for you. He says, "greater love hath no man than this, that a man lay down his life for his friends." (John xv. .) *That* is what He did for you. Can you see it ? Look at your Saviour crucified upon the cross, crowned with the sharp thorns, bleeding and suffering unto death for you. Is it not wonderful that you may say, "This is *my* Friend"?

Our Brother.

" He is not ashamed to call them brethren."
HEB. ii.

SOMETIMES people do not like it to be known if they have relations not so well off as themselves, and do not care to mention them. How different this is from the Lord Jesus ! He is the Son of God, the King of kings, and yet He is not ashamed to call us brethren. He came down to earth on purpose to be made like us in everything (Heb. ii.   ), so that He might be our brother. He is our good, kind, strong Elder Brother, and He will be to us everything you can think of about the very best brother you ever heard of.

What a difference it makes to the summer holidays when a dear elder brother comes home! And if a great home trouble comes, who is wanted so much as the elder brother who feels it all because it is his sorrow too, and yet knows what to do and how to help the others through the dark time? So it is Jesus who can make all your happiest times happier still, and yet He is the Brother born for adversity (Prov. xvii.   ), who comes to comfort and help us as no one else can, when we are in trouble.

Perhaps you think, "Oh how I should like to know that Jesus is *my* Brother!" If He is your Saviour, He will be to you all that every one of His other beautiful names tells you He is. But He has told us something which should help you to lay hold of this one. When the multitude

sat about Him, listening to His words
(Mark iii.   ), He looked round
about on them and said "Behold My
mother and My brethren! For whosoever shall do the will of God, the
same is My brother, and My sister,
and My mother." Doing the will of
God is just trying to do what He tells
you and what pleases Him. And
Jesus knows if you are really wishing
and trying to do this. And if you are,
that shows you are His little brother
or His little sister, for He says so.
And although He is the Mighty God,
He is not ashamed to call you so,
and you may say:

> Christ is my Father and my Friend,
>   My Brother and my Love;
> My Head, my Hope, my Counsellor,
>   My Advocate above.

Our Redeemer.

"I know that my Redeemer liveth."
JOB xix.

REDEEMING means buying back something that has been sold or fallen into the power of an enemy. When Adam and Eve disobeyed God and obeyed the devil, it was like selling themselves to him to be his servants instead of God's. For it says, "Know ye not that to whom ye yield yourselves servants to obey, his servants ye are to whom ye obey?" (Rom. vi.   .) And so all their children were sold too, "sold under sin" (Rom. vii.   ); and every one of them, you and I as well as the rest, have done the same thing, disobeyed God.

God says to us all, " Ye have sold yourselves for nought " (Isa. lii.   ). We could never redeem our souls ourselves, for we have nothing to do it with. And no one can do it for us (Ps. xlix.   ); all the silver and gold in the world would not be enough to redeem only one soul. Nothing but Jesus Christ's own blood could do it (1 Pet. i.   ). He saw that there was no one else to do it (Isa. lix.   ), and so "in His love and in His pity He redeemed us" (Isa. lxiii.   ). That is, He gave His own blood as the price of buying us back from Satan, taking us out of his service and out of his power, and buying us to be God's own children and His own happy little servants. And now He says to you, " Ye are not your own, for ye are bought with a price." (1 Cor. vi.   .) How we ought to thank

Him for this ! You see it is not something that we *hope* He will do for us, but something that He really *has done* for us and that can never be undone. And so even now we ought to echo the song of the saints around the throne, and say " Thou wast slain, and hast redeemed us to God by Thy blood." (Rev. v.   .) He means us to know that He is our Redeemer, for He says, " thou shalt know that I the Lord am thy Saviour and thy Redeemer." (Isa. lx.   .) When you are quite sure a thing is true, you say " I *know*." You are quite sure it is true that Jesus has redeemed us, because God's word tells us so in a great many places (Eph. i.   ; Heb. ix.   ; Luke i.   ) ; and you are quite sure that He has risen from the dead and is " alive for evermore " (Rev. i.   ), and so you may say

without fear, "I *know* that my Redeemer liveth." And the Lord Jesus
answers, "Fear not, for I have
redeemed thee; thou art Mine." (Isa.
xliii.   .)

> I could not do without Thee,
>   O Saviour of the lost !
> Whose wondrous love redeemed me
>   At such tremendous cost.
> Thy righteousness, Thy pardon,
>   Thy precious blood, must be
> My only hope and comfort,
>   My glory and my plea!

Our Master.

"Jesus saith unto her, Mary. She turned herself, and saith unto Him, Rabboni; which is to say, Master."—JOHN xx.

I SHOULD think no one ever could have been happier than Mary was that moment when she said " Master !" But every one who says " Master," and *means it*, must be happy too ; for we do not care to call Jesus " Master" until we love Him, and loving Him always makes people happy.

When we have learnt the sweet words "my Saviour" and "my Redeemer," because we believe that Jesus has saved us and bought us with His precious blood, then we are sure to want to call Him "my Master." "I

want to do something for Jesus " is one
of the first wishes that rises up in our
hearts when we see what He has done
for us, and perhaps it is one of the
surest proofs that we do love Him.
We feel like the Queen of Sheba when
she said, "Happy are these thy servants" (1 Kings x.   ).   And when
we have tried a little bit of His service
we are very glad to say "O Lord, truly
I am Thy servant."   (Ps. cxvi.   .)

But it is the Master Himself that
makes the service sweet, and so we are
gladder still when we just look up to
Him and say, like Mary, "Master!"
When we say that word to Him it
makes it all so real.   For we have not
only to look back at a dying Saviour
but to look up at a living one.   When
Mary said it, He had come up out
of the tomb never to die any more
(Rom. vi.   ), but always to live for

us ; and when we call Him by that name it may remind us that He is risen, and is really alive now, and that He says, "because I live ye shall live also." (John xiv.   .)

He has given a beautiful answer to every one who loves Him enough to call Him by this name. He says, " Ye call Me Master and Lord, and ye say well." (John xiii.   .) So He likes to hear us say it, and values the love of the poor little sinful heart that yet looks up and says, " I love my Master." (Exod. xxi.   .)

> I love, I love my Master,
>   I will not go out free !
> He loves me, oh so lovingly,
>   He is so good to me !
>
> I love, I love my Master,
>   He shed His blood fcr me,
> To ransom me from Satan's power,
>   From sin's hard slavery.

I love, I love my Master,
   Oh how He worked for me !
He worked out God's salvation,
   So great, so full, so free.

My Master, O my Master,
   If I may work for Thee,
And tell out Thy salvation,
   How happy shall I be !
            ELLEN P. SHAW.

———

For He hath met my longing
   With word of golden tone,
That I shall serve for ever
   Himself, Himself alone.

" Shall serve Him," and " for ever ":
   O hope most sure, most fair !
The perfect love outpouring
   In perfect service there !

Rejoicing and adoring,
   Henceforth my song shall be;
I love, I love my Master,
   I will not go out free !
            F. R. H.

₊ These three last verses are added since their writer went away to " serve Him day and night in His temple."

Our Physician.

"They that be whole need not a physician, but they that are sick."—MATT. ix.

HOW is it that some people care so very much about these beautiful names of Christ, and others do not care at all about them? It just depends upon whether the Holy Spirit has opened our eyes to see that we are in want of exactly the very thing that Jesus is called. That is what makes all the difference.

People who think they have nothing the matter with them do not wish for a doctor. If you heard that there was a wonderful man come to the neighbourhood who could cure consumption, I don't suppose you would think twice about it, you who have good strong lungs, and can run, and sing, and laugh! But if you had a dreadful cough, and had seen people shake their heads and whisper, "Ah, poor child, I'm afraid it is consumption!" you would want to hear everything you could about this doctor; and when they kept telling you how clever he was and how many people he had cured, I think you would want very much to go to him and be cured too.

Now every one of us is born into the world with a disease in our souls called sin (Rom. iii.   ); "and sin, when it is finished, bringeth forth death." (James i.   .) And the very worst sign of this disease is when we do not feel it, and do not know that we have it. (Rev. iii.   .)

There is only One who can heal us, and if He does not heal us we never

can be healed at all (Acts iv.   );
that is Jesus, the Good Physician; and
as He never sent any one away without
healing who came to Him on earth
(Matt. xii.   ), so He never sends
away any one (John vi.   ) who
comes to Him now to be healed of the
plague of sin. He "healeth all thy
diseases." (Ps. ciii.   .)

It is a great step towards healing
when we are shown that we do want
the Physician. Then we may come
at once to Him, no matter at all how
bad we feel, and say, "Heal my soul,
for I have sinned against Thee" (Ps.
xli.   ); and then He says, "I am
the Lord that healeth thee." (Exod.
xv.   .)

But suppose you do not feel so very
bad as all that, what then? Well, then
you must just believe that God knows
better than you, and that you *are* a

sinner and need healing, although you
don't feel it.　And then you must not
wait to feel your sinfulness ; if you do
Satan will be very clever in contriving
to hide it from you, so that you may
not come to Jesus at all.　So don't
wait for that, nor for anything, but
come and tell the Lord Jesus that,
though you do not yet *feel* much about
it, yet you *know* you need to be saved
and healed, and ask Him to be your
Good Physician, and to undertake your
case just as you are ; and then you
may say, " Heal me, O Lord, and I
shall be healed " (Jer. xvii.　) ; for
" with His stripes we are healed."
(Isa. liii.　.)

Our Substitute.

"Christ also hath once suffered for sins, the Just for the unjust, that He might bring us to God."—I Pet. iii.

WE do not find the word "substitute" in the Bible, but the sense of it comes over and over again. It means one person put in another person's place, or one thing put instead of another.

There was a little girl of three years old, who showed that she understood perfectly about the Lord Jesus being our Substitute. She put her little hands together and said, "I thank You, Jesus, that You was punished instead of me!" That is it! the Lord Jesus taking our place, and punished instead of us. That was why He suffered; He was

the Just one, that is, perfectly good;
and we are the unjust, that is, sinful
and bad; and so He suffered for our
sins, the Just one suffering instead of
us, the unjust ones.

There are many pictures of this in
the Bible.   One is when Judah, the
elder brother, wanted to save Benjamin
from being kept as a slave in Egypt.
He begged hard that he might take
his brother's place, and stay " instead of
the lad." (Gen. xliv.   .)   That was
offering to be his substitute.   When an
Israelite had sinned he was to bring a
clean animal to be killed and offered
for him ; and when he put his hand on
the head of the burnt offering it was
"accepted for him." (Lev. i.   .)
That was to teach him that Some One
must suffer and shed blood for his sin,
and that His death would be accepted
instead of his being punished.

The Lord Jesus was wounded for our transgressions, and was bruised for our iniquities; that is, He was wounded and bruised *instead* of our being punished for them. (Isa. liii.   .) And because we were like sheep going astray Jesus was led like a sheep to the slaughter, instead, always in-stead, of us! Dear children, when you hear or read the story of the cross, think of this, that Jesus was your Substitute as He hung there in all that agony; He bore it all for love of you, and for your sins, and *instead* of you!

> Oh think of His sorrow!
> That we may know
> His wondrous love
> In His wondrous woe.

Our Shepherd.

"Our Lord Jesus, that great Shepherd of the sheep."—HEB. xiii.

HERE is a little lesson for you, all in threes. Jesus Christ is the Good Shepherd, and the Great Shepherd, and the Chief Shepherd. And these three names tell us of His death, His resurrection, and His ascension.

For, as the Good Shepherd He laid down His life for the sheep (John x.); as the Great Shepherd He was brought again from the dead (Heb. xiii.); and as the Chief Shepherd He is now gone up on high, and shall appear when He comes again. (1 Pet. v. .)

He laid down His life that He might

give us a crown of life. (Rev. ii.   .)
He was raised that we might be justi-
fied (Rom. iv.   ), that is, accounted
righteous before God, so that He might
give us the crown of righteousness
(2 Tim. iv.   ); and He is coming
again to give us a crown of glory
that fadeth not away. (1 Pet. v.   .)
So the three promised crowns seem
linked with these three beautiful names
of Jesus, who is both our Shepherd and
our King.

And now think a little about what
"Shepherd" means for *you*. It means
that you have Some One to belong to,
that you are not your own. (1 Cor.
vi.   .)

It means that you have Some One to
take care of you, Some One who will
watch you and will not let you get lost.
(Luke xv.   .)

It means that you have Some One

who feeds you and will not let you starve, and if you keep near Him He will not let you be hungry at all. (Ezek. xxxiv. .)

It means that you have Some One who knows you and calls you by name. (John x. .)

It means that this One loves you so much that He laid down His life for you. (ver. .)

It means that He came on purpose to give you life, and life more abundantly (ver.), that is, that you should not be a just-alive sort of Christian, but a strong, bright, happy one, as full of life as the lambs look when they are bounding about on a sunny May morning.

And it means that He will not let any one pluck you out of His hand, and that He has given His promise that you shall never perish. (ver. .)

Now what can you want more? Should you not say, "the Lord is my Shepherd, I shall not want" (Ps. xxiii.); and will you not sing—

To praise our Shepherd's care,
  His wisdom, love, and might,
Your loudest, loftiest songs prepare,
  And bid the world unite.

Supremely good and great,
  He tends His blood-bought fold ;
He stoops, though throned in highest state
  The feeblest to uphold.

He hears their softest plaint,
  He sees them when they roam ;
And if His meanest lamb should faint,
  His bosom bears it home.

REV. W. H. HAVERGAL.

Our Passover.

"Christ our Passover is sacrificed for us."—
1 Cor. v.

THAT was a terrible night when the last of the ten plagues fell upon Pharaoh and his land. How would you have felt if you had been one of the firstborn, and had heard Moses proclaim that about midnight the Lord would go out (Exod. xi.   ), and all the firstborn in Egypt should die! Would you not have made haste to ask if there was not some way to escape being smitten? And would you not have been very glad and comforted to hear that there was a way by which you might be quite safe?

It seemed a very strange way. A

lamb was to be killed and eaten that evening, and the blood was to be sprinkled on the door posts. And God said : "When I see the blood I will pass over you." (Exod. xii.   .) People might have said : " But we don't understand ! *why* shall we be safe inside when the blood is sprinkled ?" Their not understanding did not matter at all ; God had said it, and that was enough.   Those that believed His word and took shelter under it were safe from the Destroyer ; but as for all the Egyptians who had no blood sprinkled, " there was not a house where there was not one dead."

God does not say now, " the firstborn shall die," but He says " the soul that sinneth it shall die." (Ezek. xviii.   .) And have not you and I sinned ? But Christ our Passover is sacrificed for us. So He says, " Behold

the Lamb of God which taketh away
the sin of the world." (John i.   .)
By His own blood (Heb. ix.   ),
as of a lamb (1 Pet. i.   ), He
has obtained redemption and salvation for us. Nothing else can wash
away our sins (Heb. ix.   ; Rev.
i.   ), so nothing else could save us.
This holy Lamb of God has been slain;
that was done long ago, and now we
have only to take shelter under His
precious blood, believing what God
says about it, and we are safe. We do
not have to wait till we can quite understand about it, and God does not wait
for *us* to see; but He says, "when
I see the blood I will pass over you."
No destroyer shall touch the soul that
believes God's word about Jesus and
His precious blood, and takes shelter
under that.

Our Intercessor.

"It is Christ that died, yea rather, that is risen again, who is even at the right hand of God, who also maketh intercession for us."—ROM. viii.

HERE are four wonderful steps, rising one above another. As we stand on each one we see more and more reason for happy confidence in our Lord Jesus Christ. The first is that He died for us. But if He had remained in the grave we could never have known that God had accepted His great atonement for us. So the next step of confidence is that He is risen again, so that He is our living Saviour who says, "Because I live, ye shall live also." (John xiv. .) The next is that He is even at the right hand of God, in all His power and glory, preparing a place for us, and by His Spirit preparing us for it.

Jesus dying, risen, and gone up to heaven, all for us! What could we think of more? Yet His wonderful love goes farther still, for He " also maketh intercession for us." That means, He is praying for us. One would have thought that when He went back to heaven, after all His suffering for us on earth, He would have done enough for us, and would have something else to do than be thinking about us any more. But as long as one of His dear children lives on earth, He will go on praying for each one to the end, even as He loves each one to the end (John xiii.   ); for " He *ever* liveth to make intercession for us." (Heb. vii.   .)

Think now, Jesus is praying for you to-day! Perhaps you have thought very little about Him, and grieved His loving heart, and only said a few words of cold prayers without really praying to Him at all; and He has been praying for you all the time!

Would you like to know for certain that He prays for *you?* Then see what He says in that beautiful last prayer of His on earth: " neither pray I for these alone, but for *all* them which shall believe on Me through their word." (John xvii.   .) So if you are " one of these little ones which believe in Me " (Matt. xviii.   ), Jesus prays for you as certainly as He did for Peter when He said " I have prayed for thee."   (Luke xxii.   .)

The Unspeakable Gift.

"Thanks be unto God for His unspeakable Gift."—2 COR. ix.

"THE things which are freely given to us of God" are so many and so great that we cannot know them all unless He gives us the Holy Spirit to make us know them. (1 Cor. ii. .) Once two young friends of mine set to work to make a list of all God's gifts mentioned in the Bible. They found 530 gifts, and wrote them out in a scroll, and it was more than two yards long in three columns, and in small writing too! Suppose you try and make a list at least one yard long!

What will you put down as the best gift of all? Here is the answer :

"God so loved the world, that *He gave His only begotten Son*, that whosoever believeth in Him should not perish, but have everlasting life." (John iii.   .)

All the other good gifts from our Father (James i.   ) come through this first great Gift, Jesus Himself. For He received gifts for us (Ps. lxviii.   ), and now He is sending them down to us, daily loading us with benefits (ver.   ).

Unless we are very careless and ungrateful indeed, we always care about a gift. " A gift is as a precious stone in the eyes of him that hath it." (Prov. xvii.   .) Oh what must God think of those who do not care about the most precious Gift He could possibly have given us ! Dear ones, have *you* cared for this wonderful Gift ? Have *you* ever thanked God for giving you His own dear Son ? Think of His

having given you Jesus to be to you
all that these beautiful names describe.
Think how He did not merely give
Him, but "gave Him up for us all."
(Rom. viii.   .) Gave Him up all
the thirty-three long years, gave Him up
to be scourged and crucified ! What
would any one think of you if they gave
you a magnificent present, that cost
them a very great deal to part with,
and you never said "Thank you!"
Oh what must God think if you do not
thank Him for giving the Son of His
love !

But if you do thank Him, what does
that show?   What does it show when
you say " Oh thank you very much !"
for a birthday present?   Does it not
show the giver that you believe it is
meant for you, and that you have taken
it for your own?   And then he leaves
it with you. and it *is* your own.   Is

there a little faint heart who is saying,
" Oh I *should* like to know that Jesus
is mine "?   He is God's gift to every
one who will accept Him ; so now you
just go and kneel alone before God,
and thank Him for His unspeakable
Gift ; and that will show that you
have accepted Him, and that He *is*
yours.

> I gave My life for thee,
>   My precious blood I shed
> That thou might'st ransomed be,
>   And quickened from the dead.
> I gave My life for thee :
> What hast thou given for Me ?

Our Leader.

"Behold I have given Him for a witness to the people, a Leader and commander to the people."—Isa. lv.

OUR Heavenly Father knew that we could never find our way to heaven by ourselves. He knew too that we should never find even a little bit of the right way for ourselves. So He gave us a Leader. It would have been a great deal if He had sent an angel to lead us ; but in His great love to us He did much more than that, He sent Jesus down to us and said, "Behold I have given *Him* for a Leader."

Those who want to get to the top of very high mountains in Switzerland are anxious to have the very best guide they can hear of. Very often they write to a firstrate guide months beforehand to make sure, and he engages himself, so that when they come to begin their climb the guide is all ready for them. Now we did not engage our heavenly Guide, but God knew how much we should need Him. So He engaged the Lord Jesus to be our Leader ages before we were born. And so, now that you are, I hope, beginning the upward path, Jesus is there, keeping God's promise, and ready to be your Leader.

We want inside leading and outside leading, and Jesus does both. The inside leading comes first, for He leads us to God as our Father. If He did not we never should come near at all, but always be far off, for He says, "no man cometh unto the Father but by

Me." (John xiv.   .) Then He leads us in the way of righteousness (Prov. viii.   ), that is, He leads us to do what is right.   He does not only lead all His people in general like a flock (Ps. lxxx.   ), but He calls each of us by name and leads us.   (John x.   .) So you may say like David, "He leadeth *me*." (Ps. xxiii.   .)

Then there is the outside leading, sometimes leading you to very pleasant places (Ps. xvi.   ), and sometimes leading you where you do not like to go.   But if Jesus really is your Leader He will always lead you by the right way. (Ps. cvii.   .)   He never makes a mistake in arranging for His children. He leads gently as well as rightly, like Jacob, who said he would lead on softly, according as the children should be able to endure.   (Gen. xxxiii.   .) And He always leads safely (Ps.

lxxviii.   ); so that we need not
fear.

He Himself was led as a sheep to
the slaughter. (Acts viii.   .) So He
knows how to lead His lambs till He
brings them safe to heaven. And still
He will be their Leader, for the Lamb
which is in the midst of the throne
shall feed them, and lead them unto
living fountains of waters, and God
shall wipe away all tears from their
eyes. (Rev. vii.   .)

Jesus, loving Saviour,
　　Only Thou dost know
All that may befall us
　　As we onward go.
So we humbly pray Thee,
　　Take us by the hand,
Lead us ever upward
　　To the Better Land.

Our Commander.

" Behold, I have given Him for a witness to the people, a leader and Commander to the people."—Isa. lv.

IF Jesus is our Leader, He must be our Commander too.

When God meant to bring the Israelites into the promised land He set Joshua over them to lead them out and bring them in (Num. xxvii.   ); and when Joshua was made their leader the people said, " all that thou commandest us we will do." (Josh. i.   .)

Are you ready to say that to the Lord Jesus? Does it seem very hard? Are you afraid He may command you something you would not like to do?

It would be not only very hard, but quite impossible, to do what He commands, if it were not for two things.

The first is that He has promised to write His laws in our hearts (Heb. viii.   ); which means that He will make our hearts willing and glad to keep them. And He gives His Holy Spirit to enable us to keep them.

And the second is, that love makes all the difference to obedience. When sailors have a good commander of their ship they like doing what he wants done. The hardship to them would be to be prevented from doing it. So, if we love our Commander, we shall *want* to do what He bids us. Suppose you had been there that last, sweet, solemn evening, when He had the last long talk with His disciples, just before He went to Gethsemane, and had heard Him say, "If ye love

Me, keep My commandments" (John
xiv.   ), don't you think you would
have wished to keep them? Would
you have thought it hard then?

Look in those beautiful chapters
(John xiv.   , and xv.   ,) and find
out for yourself what Jesus promises to
those who keep His commandments;
and then see what St. John says about
them in his First Epistle (chap. v.   );
for, after all, He never commands us
one single thing but what will make
us happy if we only do *exactly* what
He tells us. They are "for our good,
always." (Deut. vi.   .) If everybody kept them, everybody would be
happy, as happy as the angels (Ps. ciii.
      ); for " blessed " (that means very
happy *indeed*) "is the man that de-
lighteth greatly in His commandments." (Ps. cxii.   .) Ask Him to
make you love Him so much that you

may say, " I will delight myself in Thy commandments, which I have loved." (Ps. cxix.   .)

> Just to ask Him what to do
>   All the day,
> And to make you quick and true
>   To obey.
> Just to know the needed grace
>   He bestoweth,
> Every bar of time and place
>   Overfloweth.
> Just to take thy orders straight
>   From the Master's own command.
> Blessèd day ! when thus we wait
>   Always at our Sovereign's hand.

Our Head.

"The Head, even Christ."—EPH. iv.

HERE is another name of Christ
as the Gift of God; for God
"gave Him to be Head over all things
to the Church, which is His body."
(Eph. i.   .) Perhaps you never
thought before of Jesus being your
Head! But you will find great help
in thinking about everything that God
has told us about Him.

If He is our Head, and we are His
body, it is very plain that we cannot
do without Him. What could your
hands and feet do if they were not
joined to your head? so the Lord
Jesus might well say, "without Me
ye can do nothing." (John xv.   .)

If He is our Head, you cannot grow without Him; and more than that, you cannot live without Him, any more than you could if your head were cut off. There is only death in the soul that is without Jesus, no real life at all: for "he that hath the Son hath life; and he that hath not the Son of God hath not life." (1 John v.   .)

I said you could not grow without Him. That is why some of you do not seem to grow better and brighter and stronger little Christians; it is when you are "not holding the Head," (Col. ii.   ,) (that is, not keeping close to Jesus) that you do not get on. He does not want you to be like a poor little cripple or dwarf, but to grow up into Him in all things. (Eph. iv.   .)

Let me then be always growing,
  Never, never standing still;
Listening, learning, better knowing
  Thee and Thy most holy will.

If Jesus is your Head, then you are the body of Christ, and members in particular. (1 Cor. xii.   .) Yes, each of you "*in particular*"; not everybody in general! And even if you are a very little member, or a very feeble member (ver.   ), you are "necessary," and Jesus would not do without you, any more than your head would choose to do without one of your fingers or feet. Fancy your saying, "Oh, I don't care much about this foot; you may cut it off if you like!" Just so the Lord Jesus cares about every little member who is joined to Him, and will not let it be cut off from His body; the Head cannot say to the feet, I have no need of you.

(ver.   .)   Now is it not a very precious name which teaches us such a precious truth?

Now you will understand better how Jesus feels for us; for if your little finger is hurt, your head does not have to be told! you know about it, and feel it, and cry out, in an instant. So if the least little member of Christ suffers, He knows, and feels, and sympathises, because " Christ is the Head." (Eph. v.   .)

> Make Thy members every hour
>   For Thy blessèd service meet ;
> Earnest tongues, and arms of power,
>   Skilful hands, and hastening feet,
> Ever ready to fulfil
> All Thy word, and all Thy will.

Our Light.

" I am the Light of the world ; he that fol-
loweth Me shall not walk in darkness, but
shall have the light of life."—JOHN viii.

SOME people don't see what they
want with this Light ! they think
their own eyes and common sense, and
what they call "the light of reason,"
are quite enough for them.   But Jesus
says, "Take heed therefore that the
light that is in thee be not darkness"
(Luke xi.   ); and, "If therefore
the light that is in thee be darkness,
how great is that darkness !" (Matt. vi.
    .)   For Jesus Himself is the true
Light (John i.   ), and if we have
not the true Light of course we can't
see right.

The Holy Spirit very often shows us the darkness first, so as to make us seek the Light. A young girl said to me, " I can't see my way through the sins." It was a great thing that the good Spirit was showing her the darkness. Nothing is worse than not to know that we are "poor, and miserable, and blind " (Rev. iii.   ), because then we do not want the Light. Now if you feel something like that girl, just bring the sins to Jesus, bring the darkness to the Light, and in His light you shall see light. (Ps. xxxvi.   .) We *cannot* be in the dark when we come close to a bright light ; there cannot be darkness in our hearts when we open the door and let the Lord Jesus come in.

Some of you know well enough already what the difference is, and how true it comes that " Christ shall give thee light." (Eph. v.   .) How the puzzles are made clear, and the doubts all go we don't know where, and the shadows flee away, and everything seems bright, when we really come to Jesus! Ever so many of you are saying, I know, as you read this, "Yes, yes! that is just it!" Why not all of you?

This is one of the special things that God gave Jesus to be: "a Light of the Gentiles." (Isa. xlii.   .) Old Simeon was so glad when he saw the Light that he was ready to die at once. (Luke ii.   .) There are three names of Jesus in that beautiful little song of Simeon's, "Lord, now lettest Thou." Think about them next time you sing it; and ask Jesus to be your Salvation, your Light, and your Glory. Then, when He lets you depart in peace, "the Lord shall be unto thee an Ever-

lasting Light, and thy God thy Glory."
(Isa. lx.   .)

It was not always light with me; for many a
   sinful year
I walked in darkness, far from Thee; but Thou
   hast brought me near,
And washed me in Thy precious blood, and
   taught me by Thy grace,
And lifted up on my poor soul the brightness
   of Thy face.

My Saviour died in darkness that I might live
   in light,
He closed His eyes in death that mine might
   have the heavenly sight;
He gave up all His glory to bring it down to me,
And took the sinner's place that He the sinner's
   Friend might be.

His Spirit shines upon His word, and makes
   it sweet indeed,
Just like a shining lamp held up beside me as
   I read;
And brings it to my mind again alone upon my
   bed,
Till all abroad within my heart the love of God
   is shed.

Our Life.

" When Christ, who is our Life, shall appear,
then shall ye also appear with Him in glory."
Col. iii.

ONCE I asked a poor French girl
if she was afraid to die.   She
shrugged her shoulders, and said, " Ah,
death, death ! it is terrible, terrible ! "
She was quite right. For death *is* terrible
in itself, and the second death (Rev.
xx.   ) is more terrible still.   And if
persons have never felt afraid to die,
I am afraid it shows they do not
know anything about it, like a child
fast asleep in a burning house.

But just because death is terrible
Christ our Life is precious.   This is
good news for every one who is afraid

to die. Jesus Christ gives us life, not
for trying, not even for asking, but only
just for believing on Him! He says,
"Verily, verily, I say unto you, He
that believeth on Me hath everlasting
life." (John vi.   .) Would Jesus have
said that, and not mean it? Would He
have said that if you believe in Him
you have everlasting life, if He only
meant that He would perhaps give it
you and perhaps not? And would He
have said " *everlasting* life," if it was a
life that you might lose to-morrow and
that might *not* last? Take the gladness of the good news, and believe
that Jesus meant what He said, and
meant it for you! And then you need
not fear death any more than you fear
to go to sleep, for death is only falling asleep for those who are safe in
Jesus. It will be only like going to
sleep in your little bed, and waking

up in a different place, the most beautiful place you can imagine!

But Jesus does more than give us life. He *is* our Life. Thinking of Him as our Head will help you to understand this. Your finger, for instance, is not a separate little live thing; it lives because it is joined to your head, and to what a little girl called your *"think"*; and it is because your head is alive that your finger is alive. Just so Jesus says, "because I live, ye shall live also." (John xiv.   .)

And how long will Jesus live? He says, "Behold I am alive for evermore." (Rev. i.   .) So how long will every little member of Christ live? Must it not be "for evermore" too? So you see the promise of everlasting life is sure because "Christ being raised from the dead dieth no more." (Rom.

vi.   .)   He died for us, that whether
we wake or sleep we should live together with Him. (1 Thess. v.   .)
Do you not see? If you believe in
Jesus, your life depends on His life,
and it is "hid" with Him. (Col. iii.
    .)   And do you think Satan could
get at what is hid with Christ?   Must
it not be quite safe there ?

Jesus, Thy life is mine !
Dwell evermore in me;
And let me see
That nothing can untwine
My life from Thine.

Jesus, my life is Thine,
And evermore shall be
Hidden in Thee !
For nothing can untwine
Thy life from mine.

©ur 𝕽ock.

" Lead me to the Rock that is higher than I."—Ps. lxi.

THERE are so many thoughts about Jesus as our Rock, that we can only find room for a very few of them.

First, He is the smitten Rock (Num. xx.   ); for He was smitten of God (Isa. liii.   ), and smitten of man too, as we read in the solemn story of His sufferings.   Smitten, like the rock in the thirsty desert, with a rod ; for it says, " they shall smite the Judge of Israel with a rod upon the cheek." (Micah v.   .)   Smitten that the stream of life might flow forth for you and me.

Secondly, He is the cleft Rock. God said to Moses, " Behold, there is a place by Me, and thou shalt stand upon a rock." (Exod. xxxiii.   .) And He put him in a cleft of the rock, and covered him with His hand, while His glory passed by. You know how you like to have a place by one you love, and what an honour it is to have a place by some one who is great or noble !   So, when God sets our feet upon the Rock (Ps. xl.   ), it is a place by Him, a happy place, and an honourable place. It is a safe place too, not only safe from the great enemy now ; but when the great and terrible day of the Lord comes (Joel ii. ·   ), and His glory is more than the unsheltered ones can bear, those in the cleft of the Rock will have nothing to fear.

Thirdly, He is the Higher Rock.

When the tide is beginning to come in, it would be no use standing on a rock no higher than yourself. The waves would very soon dash over that, and drown you. But if you climb up to a higher rock, ever so much above your head, the waves can never reach you. No matter how furiously they roll in, you are just as safe as if there was not such a thing as a wave at all! So when God leads you to the Higher Rock, that is, when His grace draws you to come to Jesus (John vi.   ), you are safe!

Fourthly, He is the strong Rock. (Ps. xxxi.   .) David knew what it was to dwell in rocks, to be out of the way of Saul (1 Sam. xxiii.   ) ; and so he said, " Be Thou my strong habitation (margin, a rock of habitation), whereunto I may continually resort." (Ps. lxxi.   .) That is just what

Jesus is, a strong Rock, where we may always go to be safe out of the way of our enemy, Satan.

Fifthly, He is a Rock of offence. (1 Pet. ii.   .) It is very sad and solemn to read this, but it is true. Those who do not like to come to Jesus as the Rock of salvation (Deut. xxxii.   ) will know some day what its terrible meaning is. But may all my little readers, and older ones too, be like the coneys, so wise though so feeble, because they make their houses in the rocks. (Prov. xxx.   .) Remember that the Lord Jesus calls those who love Him His doves, that are in the clefts of the rock. (Cant. ii.   .) And if you are like the coneys and the doves in this, then He says to you " Let the inhabitants of the Rock sing !" (Isa. xlii.   .)

Our Righteousness.

"This is His name whereby He shall be called, THE LORD OUR RIGHTEOUS-NESS."—JER. xxiii.

THIS is always printed in large capitals in our Bibles. And no wonder, for it is so very important. You see, righteousness is something that we must have, or we cannot go to heaven, any more than you could go to a grand royal entertainment without a proper dress. They would not let you in if you were all in rags, you know that well enough; nobody but a lunatic would attempt to go in that condition.

All our righteousnesses, that is, all the good things we ever did or tried to do, are filthy rags. (Isa. lxiv. .) It is no use trying to make them out to be anything cleaner and better; if God says they are filthy rags, they *are* so.

Even these filthy rags do not cover us; the very best "filthy rag" garment that ever anybody tried to make for himself is so full of holes, and is so scanty, that it cannot cover us. God says, "their webs" (that is, what they try to spin and weave for themselves out of their own goodness) "shall not become garments, neither shall they cover themselves with their own works." (Isa. lix.   .) What will you do without something better?

When the king came in to see the guests, he saw there a man which had not on a wedding garment. He had no excuse, for the king himself provided the garments. So he was to be bound hand and foot, and cast into outer darkness. (Matt. xxii.   .) You see, he had to have it *on*; the garment was there for him, and he must have known about it, only he did not choose to accept it and put it on. Even so, we must accept "the righteousness of God which is by faith of Jesus Christ unto all and *upon* all them that believe." (Rom. iii.   .) For believing God's word about it *is* putting it on; and then Jesus Christ Himself is made unto us righteousness. (1 Cor. i.   .)   And then you may say, " I will greatly rejoice in the Lord, my soul shall be joyful in my God: for He hath clothed me with the garments of salvation, He hath covered me with the robe of righteousness." (Isa. lxi.   .)

Does this seem rather dry to you? It would not seem dry if you knew you were just going to be called to stand before God, and that you must either stand in filthy rags or in the

perfectly beautiful and spotless robe.
What if the call came, and found you
hesitating whether you would put it on
or not! How you would wish then
that you knew Jesus to be the Lord
your Righteousness! Ask the Holy
Spirit *now* to show you all that He
means in this wonderful name, so
that you may say, " In the Lord have
I righteousness and strength." (Isa.
xlv.   .)

Your righteousness, as filthy rags,
   Must all relinquished be,
And only Jesu's precious blood
   Must be your plea.

Fear not to trust His simple word,
   So sweet, so tried, so true !
Righteous in Him, for evermore :
   Yes, even you !

Our Captain.

" The Captain of their salvation."
HEB. ii.

THE children of Israel had been vexed and oppressed by the Ammonites for eighteen years. (Jud. x. .) They were " sore distressed," and did not know what to do, because the Ammonites were gathered together against them, and they had no one to begin to fight for them. (ver. .) At last they thought of Jephthah, a mighty man of valour, whom they had treated very badly. They sent and said to him, " Come, and be our captain." (Jud. xi. .) But Jephthah said : " Did ye not hate me and expel me out of my father's house ? And why are ye come unto me now, when ye are in distress?" That was the very reason why they had come! and so they said, " *Therefore* we turn again to thee now, that thou mayest go with us, and fight against the children of Ammon." Jephthah did not mean not to go, but only to remind them of their unkindness. For he went with them, and fought for them and delivered them.

I wonder whether you have ever yet found out what strong and terrible enemies you have! If persons have never found sin and self and Satan trying to make them do wrong instead of right, and been oppressed and distressed about it, I am afraid they have been fast asleep or something worse, "dead in trespasses and sins." (Eph. ii.   .) Just as a dead Israelite would not have felt vexed and oppressed by the Ammonites' tyranny and cruelty; he would have known nothing about it.

But if you have been awake enough to say, "The good that I would I do not; but the evil that I would not, that I do" (Rom. vii.   ); then, like the Israelites, you will be glad to hear of One who is the Captain of our salvation. And though you may not have loved Him at all, and have driven the very thought of Him out of your mind, yet He is so forgiving and gracious that, as soon as ever you cry to Him for help, He will come and be your Captain.

A captain in the Queen's army sometimes has to lead his soldiers on to death. But Jesus, our Captain, only leads us on to life and victory. No one can be defeated while really following Him, for He conquers for us and in us, and makes us more than conquerors because He so loves us. (Rom. viii.　.) He has conquered all our enemies already, so we only have to pursue the defeated foes with the shout of victory. He is the Mighty God (Isa. ix.　) ; so we may say, " Behold, God Himself is with us for our Captain." (2 Chron. xiii.　.)

Captain of Israel's host, and Guide
  Of all who seek the land above,
Beneath Thy shadow we abide,
  The cloud of Thy protecting love ;
Our strength, Thy grace; our rule, Thy word ;
Our end, the glory of the Lord.

By Thine unerring Spirit led,
  We shall not in the desert stray ;
We shall not full direction need,
  Nor miss our providential way ;
As far from danger as from fear,
While love, almighty love, is near.

The Apostle of our Profession.

"Wherefore, holy brethren, partakers of the heavenly calling, consider the Apostle and high priest of our profession, Christ Jesus."— HEB. iii.

NOW let us do what we are told, and "consider" the Lord Jesus as the Apostle of our profession. Sixteen hundred and eighty-nine years before He came, Jacob prophesied of Him as "Shiloh." (Gen. xlix.   .) Shiloh means the Sent One, and "Apostle" means the same thing, "one who is sent." So when the fulness of time (that is, just the *right* time) was come, God sent forth His Son (Gal. iv.   ), sent Him to be the Saviour of the world. (1 John iv.   .)

The Lord Jesus seems to have delighted to remind the people that His Father sent Him, because that showed His Father's kindness and love. He said, "Neither came I of Myself, but He sent Me." (John viii.   .) See if you cannot make a list of thirty-seven verses in the Gospel of St. John, where He speaks of His Father having sent Him.

What was Jesus sent to do? He says, "Lo, I come . . . to do Thy will, O God" (Heb. x.   ), that is, to do what God wanted Him to do. And what was that? To give Himself for our sins, that He might deliver us from this present evil world, according to the will of God and our Father. (Gal. i.   .) And He says, "This is the Father's will which hath sent Me, that of all which He hath given Me I should lose nothing." So Jesus is the

Great Apostle sent with God's message of salvation to us, sent to do for us what God's loving heart wanted done, first to deliver us and then to keep us. Is not this worth " considering "?

Jesus, our Apostle, says, " as Thou hast sent Me into the world, even so have I sent them into the world." (John xvii.   .) He did not mean only the eleven apostles, for He says that great prayer was *not* for them alone, but for all them which should believe on Him through their word (ver.   ). So He has sent you who believe in Jesus, just as the Father sent Him.   And oh, I do so wish that some of you, some of my own dear little readers, may hear in their hearts the voice of the Lord saying, " Whom shall I send ? and who will go for us?" and answer, " Here am I ; send *me!*" (Isa. vi.   .)

There are millions who have never heard the name of Jesus; would you not like to be His ambassadors to them? Will not some of you, when you are old enough, obey His command, "Go ye into all the world, and preach the gospel to every creature!" (Matt. xxviii. .) I think it is the greatest, grandest, noblest thing you can be, a real missionary, sent into the world by our Great Apostle!

Once a young missionary was leaving home very early in the morning. It was terribly hard work to leave his mother, and when it came to the "good bye" his faith and courage failed; and he felt as if he could not go, and must give it up. Just that moment the hall door was opened, and all at once he caught sight of the beautiful morning star shining in the still dark sky; and instantly two texts

flashed into his mind.   One was, "they
that turn many to righteousness shall
shine as the stars for ever and ever."
(Dan. xii.   .)   And the other was, "*I
am the Bright and Morning Star!*"
(Rev. xxii.   .)   That promise of God
and that bright name of Jesus shone
into his heart, and gave him comfort
and strength; and he went forth to
the noble work.

   And still God says to you all, "Who
will go?"

> Who is on the Lord's side?
>   Who will serve the King?
> Who will be His helpers,
>   Other lives to bring?
> Who will leave the world's side?
>   Who will face the foe?
> Who is on the Lord's side?
>   Who for Him will go?
>   By Thy call of mercy,
>   By Thy grace Divine,
>   We are on the Lord's side;
>   Saviour, we are Thine.

Our High Priest.

"We have a great High Priest."—HEB. iv.

MOST likely this does not seem such an easy name as the rest; but I want you to try all the more to understand it, and be sure to find out all the texts.

St. Paul explains to us how everything that God commanded the Israelites about their worship was meant to teach something about Jesus Christ; and nearly all of it was to teach about His saving and cleansing us from sin.

Aaron was appointed the first high priest. Once every year there was to be a great day of atonement. (Exod. xxx.   .) Then Aaron was to kill the

goat of the sin offering (Lev. xvi.   ),
and to take its blood within the veil,
into the holy of holies, and sprinkle it
before the mercy seat. With this
blood atonement was made for the sinful souls of the people. (Lev. xvii. 11,
and Heb. ix. 22. Mind you look out
these verses!) No one was to go in
with him, and no one could help him;
he was to do it all by himself. Now
get the 9th chapter of Hebrews, and
see how St. Paul explains it. Jesus
is our High Priest (ver.   ). He did
not take the blood of goats, but His
own blood; and with this He entered
into the holy place and obtained
eternal redemption for us (ver.   ).
He does not need to do it every day
(Heb. vii.   ), nor every year
(Heb. ix.   ); but once, and only
once (ver.   ); because His blood
is so precious that that was enough

for us all and for ever. (Heb. x.   .)
No one ever had or ever can have
anything to do with this great atonement by blood ; it was *by Himself* that
He purged our sins (Heb. i.   ), and
by Him we have now received the
atonement. (Rom. v.   .) So now
we may draw near, with a true heart,
in full assurance of faith (Heb. x.   )
(that means being *quite sure*), because
Jesus is our High Priest, and God's
word tells us what He has done for us,
so that there cannot be any mistake
about it.   And He is a merciful and
faithful High Priest (Heb. ii.   ),
and knows all about our little feelings
and temptations (Heb. iv.   ) better
than any one else does.   " Let us
therefore come boldly unto the throne
of grace, that we may obtain mercy
and find grace to help in time of
need." (Heb. iv.   .)

Wonderful.

" His name shall be called Wonderful."
ISA. ix.

EVERY boy and girl knows that
names are nouns. All the other
names of Jesus are nouns. But here
is a name that is an adjective; so we
may use it not only as a name by itself, but as an adjective to all His
other names; and the more we know
Him and love Him the more we shall
delight in this.

If we know Jesus as our Saviour at
all, we shall be quite sure that He is a
Wonderful Saviour. And if we grow
in grace and in the knowledge of our
Lord and Saviour Jesus Christ (2 Pet.
iii.   ), we shall find more and more,

year by year, and even day by day, what a Wonderful Friend, and Wonderful Gift, and Wonderful High Priest, and Wonderful everything else He is.

When you see a wonderful sight don't you always want others to see it first thing? And if you cannot bring them to see it, don't you want to tell about it, try to give them an idea of it? So I think one proof that we have really found Jesus is that we shall want others to come and see (John i.) what a wonderful Saviour we have found.

Jesus is Wonderful in what He is. Even the angels must have wondered to see the Son of God, whom they all worship (Heb. i.), lying in a manger as a helpless and poor little baby. But I think they must have wondered more still when they saw " Him taken and by wicked hands

crucified and slain" (Acts ii.   ).
They must have marvelled indeed
then at the love of Christ which
passeth knowledge (Eph. iii.   ), yet
He was not dying for them but for
you. So the poorest little child may
say, "Thy love to *me* was wonderful."
(2 Sam. i.   .)

Everything that He did was
wonderful. Isaiah said that many
should be astonished at Him (Isa.
lii.   ); and I want you to see how
exactly that was fulfilled. Look in the
first seven chapters of St. Mark, and
you will see it five times mentioned
that they were astonished or amazed
at Him.

And His words were not less
wonderful, for, as Nicodemus said,
"no man ever spake like this Man."
(John vii.   .) Look in the 4th
chapter of St. Luke, and you will see

how even those who did not love Him wondered (ver.   ), and were astonished (ver.   ) and amazed (ver.   ) at His words. If we wonder at His gracious words to us now, how much more shall we wonder when we see Him on the throne of His glory, and hear His own voice say to us, " Come, ye blessed " ! (Matt. xxv.   .)

O Bringer of salvation,
   Who wondrously hast wrought,
Thyself the revelation
   Of love beyond our thought :
We worship Thee, we bless Thee,
   To Thee alone we sing ;
We praise Thee, and confess Thee
   Our gracious Lord and King !

Counsellor.

"His name shall be called Wonderful, Counsellor."—ISA. ix.

PEOPLE who think themselves very wise and clever would not care very much for this beautiful name of the Lord Jesus, for we always have to see how poor we are before we can see how precious Jesus is.

If you have found out that you are not very wise and clever, and that you sometimes makes mistakes, and say or do just what you wish afterwards you had not said or done, you will be ready to see how good it is to have a Counsellor.

How many foolish things we do! We have to say again and again, " O

God, Thou knowest my foolishness."
(Ps. lxix.   .)   And when we look
back on a day or a week, how often
we have to say, "So foolish was I."
(Ps. lxxiii.   .)   Then sometimes
we feel puzzled as to what we had
better do, and there is no one to tell
us.   And sometimes we have to give
an answer all in a minute, and there is
no time to ask any one to tell us what
to say.   These are the times for find-
ing out what God meant by saying that
"His name shall be called Counsellor."
It does not take a minute to whisper to
the Lord Jesus in your heart, asking
Him to tell you what to do or what to
say.   It is not like having to write a
letter to ask a friend's advice, and wait
to send it by post and get an answer.
The Lord Jesus is always there, and
always ready to advise you.

But it is no good having a wonderful

Counsellor unless you make use of Him. When the Moabites and Ammonites came against Jehoshaphat (2 Chron. xx.   ), he said, " neither know we what to do " ; but he did not stop there, he made use of the great Counsellor, and added, " but our eyes are upon Thee." And then, of course, God showed him exactly what to do, and saved him out of all the trouble. Now, the very next time you have to say " neither know I what to do," recollect that Jesus is your Counsellor, and look up to Him, and do not be one bit afraid but what He will, in some way or other, guide you, whether it may be the steps, or the words, or anything else, that want guiding. (Ps. xxxii.   .)

We find Jesus most of all precious as our Counsellor when we come and ask Him about the most important things of all. Sometimes we feel as if we could not possibly tell anybody what our heart is very full of, and so we go on without getting any help or counsel. Do you want to understand better about your sins being forgiven? do you want to know how to get on faster? do you want to know how to please God, and yet you have no one that you can ask about all this? Now take this name of Jesus for yourself. Jesus is come to be *your* Counsellor, and He is able to make all this clear to you far better than any one else, if you will only ask Him. Most likely He will give you the counsel by re-minding you of something that He has written already for you. He generally does this; so if you take your Bible and "watch to see what He will say unto you," (Hab. ii.   ,) you will very soon be able to say, "I will bless the

Lord, who hath given me counsel."
(Ps. xvi.   .)

Master, speak ! Thy servant heareth,
    Longing for Thy gracious word,
Longing for Thy voice that cheereth ;
    Master, let it now be heard.
I am listening, Lord, for Thee ;
What hast Thou to say to me?

Speak to me by name, O Master,
    Let me know it is to me ;
Speak, that I may follow faster,
    With a step more firm and free,
Where the Shepherd leads the flock,
In the shadow of the Rock !

The Mighty God.

"His name shall be called . . . the Mighty God."—ISA. ix.

CHILDREN do not often think of this name of Jesus ; but it is not only the grandest of them all, but one of the most comforting, even to a little child who feels afraid and begins to wonder whether, after all, it will get safe to heaven at last.

We have thought about how gracious Jesus is as our Saviour, and how loving He is as our Brother, and how kind He is as our Friend. And this is all true ; Jesus is all that ; but He is more too. Now let us think of Him as the Mighty God, and learn how great and glorious and strong our own dear

Saviour and Friend is. Now we see
why He is able to do everything for us,
and why He is so mighty to save. (Isa.
lxiii.   .)   Of course He is ! for this
same Jesus is " the Mighty God."

More than seven hundred years before
He was born as a little child His name
was foretold ; it was to be Immanuel,
and that meant, God with us.   (Isa. vii.
.)   Then, in the next chapter, God's
people were encouraged not to be afraid,
even though enemies came against
them, strong and many (Isa. viii.   ),
like the overflowing waters of a river,
because of this very name, " God with
us " (ver.   ).   Then, in the next
chapter, more still was told about the
One who was to come, and seven
names were given Him in one verse.
(Isa. ix.   .)

Even Isaiah himself must have wondered what it meant (1 Pet. i.   )

when God's Spirit made him write that
the coming Messiah should be "a
Child" and yet "the Mighty God."
And though we do not wonder in the
same way, because we know how it
came true, yet I think we shall always
wonder more and more at this mystery
of godliness. (1 Tim. iii.   .) How
we ought to thank God for thinking of
this wonderful way of saving and help-
ing and meeting the children, by being
God with us as a little child! And
how reverently we ought to speak of
the Lord Jesus when we recollect that
He is "*God* our Saviour" (Tit. i.   ,
ii.   , iii.   ). And oh how sure
we may be that He must be able to
save, and that we may trust Him to
save us! Think of this next time you
sing, "My soul doth magnify the Lord,
and my spirit hath rejoiced in *God
my Saviour.*" (Luke i.   .)

The Everlasting Father.

"His name shall be called . . . the Everlasting Father."—ISA. ix.

THIS is another name of Christ, of which you may not have thought. Perhaps He thought of it when He said to His disciples, "I will not leave you comfortless." (John xiv. .) For that word really means orphans, as you will see in the margin of your Bible. They could not be left orphans when Jesus was their Everlasting Father.

Perhaps some one will read this whose dear father has been taken away; possibly some one, still more to be pitied, who knows what it is to have a father without having a father's kindness and love and care. Surely this name of Jesus was meant to comfort you! Jesus, the Mighty God, is your Everlasting Father, always loving, never leaving. All that you ever knew or thought a dear father would be, He will be to you. It is those who are "without Christ" (Eph. ii.   ) who have the saddest orphanhood; for the children of Jesus always have His promise, "I will not leave you orphans."

How did we come to be His children? This question has a wonderful answer, far away back before the world was made, farther back than you can think,—an answer which we never could have known unless He had told us Himself. We are His children, because God gave us to Jesus. For Jesus says, "Behold I and the children which God hath given Me" (Heb. ii.   );

and, " All that the Father hath given Me shall come to Me." (John vi.   .) In His great prayer for us, He speaks seven times of our being given to Him. (John xvii.   .) We have often thought of His being God's gift to us, but did you ever think that we are God's gift to Him? But you see He says so! So this is why we are His children, and why we are so very precious to Him. See what beautiful things we find to make us trustful and happy, when we look into His word to see what He Himself says in answer to our questions!

He is bringing many sons unto glory now (Heb. ii.   ), and He is able to keep you from falling (Jude   ), and to present you faultless before the throne of His glory with exceeding joy. For He says, " Father, I will that they also, whom Thou hast given

Me, be with Me where I am, that
they may behold My glory." (John
xvii.   .)

" The *Everlasting* Father !"
O name of gentlest grace,
O name of strength and might,
Meeting the heart-need of our orphaned race
With tenderest delight !
Our Everlasting Father ! this is He
Who came in deep humility
A little child to be !

The Prince of Peace.

" His name shall be called . . . the Prince
of Peace."—ISA. ix.

SUPPOSE you go to see a grand
house. The more you walk round
it, inside and out, the better you will
understand and admire it. But as
you look first at one side and then at
another, you will get quite different
views of it, and yet it is always one
and the same house. So it is that we
get different views of the Lord Jesus,
and yet He is always " this same
Jesus." (Acts i.   .)

Now, though we are right and glad
to think of Jesus as king, reigning
gloriously already, yet we like to remember that another of His names is

Prince,—Messiah the Prince, as He was called by Gabriel. (Dan. ix.   .) This shows us another side of what He is.

For a prince is a king's son, and Jesus is the Son of God, who is the King of all the earth. (Ps. xlvii.   .)

A prince is heir to a kingdom, and so Jesus is Heir of all things (Heb. i.   ); and the time is coming when the kingdoms of this world shall become the kingdoms of our Lord and of His Christ. (Rev. xi.   .) How different the newspapers will be then, if there are any!

But a prince has royal honour now, and so it is God's will that all men should honour the Son, even as they honour the Father. (John v.   .)

A prince has other names joined to his title, and so has Jesus; and all His names show how He is the " Prince of

princes " (Dan. viii.   ), far, far beyond all others.

First, He is the Prince of Peace.
What music there is in this beautiful
name ! Does it not sound as if an
echo of the angels' song had been
caught and kept in it, waking up again
in our hearts whenever we think of
Jesus as the Prince of Peace, who
made peace in heaven (Luke xix.   )
and came to give peace on earth.
(Luke ii.   .)

Then He is the Prince of Life
(Acts iii.   ), whom God hath raised
from the dead. For God has given
Him power over all flesh, that He
should give eternal life to as many as
God has given Him (John xvii.   );
and that, you know, is all who come to
Him. (John vi.   .)

Then He is exalted to be a Prince
and a Saviour (Acts v.   ), so that

He may give repentance and forgiveness of sins.

And, last, He is the Prince of the kings of the earth. (Rev. i.   .) And this gives us a glimpse of His greatness and glory, which we do not fully see yet. But if we rejoice already in this bright and royal name of Jesus, when His glory shall be revealed we shall be glad with exceeding joy. (1 Pet. iv.   .)

O the joy to see Thee reigning,
    Thee my own belovèd Lord !
Every tongue Thy name confessing,
Worship, honour, glory, blessing
    Brought to Thee with one accord ;
Thee, my Master and my Friend,
    Vindicated and enthroned,
Unto earth's remotest end
    Glorified, adored, and owned.

Messiah.

"And after threescore and two weeks shall Messiah be cut off, but not for Himself."—DAN. ix.

PERHAPS you thought this name did not sound interesting, and had nothing to do with you. Let us see !

" Messiah " is in Hebrew the same as " Christ " in Greek ; and the English of both is "Anointed." Many times in the Old Testament God speaks of Jesus as " His Anointed." You know how kings were anointed with oil ; Queen Victoria herself was anointed with oil when she was crowned. And the high priest was always anointed with oil when he was consecrated. (Exod. xxix.

.) And sometimes the great pro-
phets were anointed before they began
their work. (1 Kings xix.   .) So the
name " Messiah " teaches us at once
that Jesus is our Prophet, Priest, and
King, all three in one.

But we never read of the Lord
Jesus being anointed with oil. Oil is
only a type of something else, and not
any good in itself. So we are told in
plain words that " God anointed Jesus
of Nazareth with the Holy Ghost and
with power." (Acts x.   .) Of course
the Lord Jesus *as God* did not need it ;
for Father, Son, and Spirit are one God.
But it was *as man,* and for our sakes,
that He received it ; and God gave it
to Him without measure. (John iii.

.)   Now turn to Psalm cxxxiii.,
and there you will see (ver.   ) how
plentifully Aaron, the high priest, was
anointed, so that the precious ointment

went down from the head to the skirts of his garments. That was to show us that the Holy Spirit, which was poured out upon the Lord Jesus, our Head, flows down from Him even to the feet, the lowest members of all. *Now* do you see how this name has to do with you, if you have to do with Jesus? The blessed Spirit, whose work it is to make us holy, is given to us because of Jesus, and comes down to us from Jesus, and reaches in holy and constant flow every one who is joined to the Lord Jesus by faith. There could be no gift of the Holy Spirit if it were not for the gift of Jesus, the Anointed One.

The name Messiah always reminds us too of God's faithfulness in sending Jesus. For it was by this name that the Jews expected Him for hundreds of years. How glad Philip must have

been when he could say, "We have
found the Messias!" (John i.   .)
Ought not we to be glad too? For
"we know that the Son of God is
come" (1 John v.   ), and we know
too that He is just as surely coming
again. (Acts i.   .) The Jews do not
believe it even yet, because the veil
is upon their heart. (2 Cor. iii.   .)
They cannot make it out, because they
know the time of which Daniel spoke
is past long ago. We ought to pray
that the veil may be taken away, that
they may see that Messiah is come,
and that He was cut off, not for Himself, but for them. And for *you!*

> Messiah's name shall joy impart
> Alike to Jew and Gentile heart;
> He bled for us, He bled for you,
> And we will sing Hosanna too!

Our Judge.

" He commanded us to preach unto the people, and to testify that it is He which was ordained of God to be the Judge of quick and dead."—Acts x.

WE must not dare to pick and choose in the Bible. (Rev. xxii.   .) It is *all* true, and will all come true ; not liking to think about any part of it does not make it any the less true.   Then is it not better to know the whole truth ?

So, in thinking of the names of Christ, we must not leave out what seems at first sight a terrible name, for it is a great truth that He will certainly come to be our Judge.   And God wishes us all to know it, for He com-

manded the apostles to preach it, and
so His ministers would be doing wrong
if they never preached about it, whether
people like it or not !

" He shall come again with glory to
judge both the quick and the dead."
Whether we are "quick," that is
"alive," when the Lord Jesus comes,
or dead, will make no difference. " For
we shall *all* stand before the judgment
seat of Christ." (Rom. xiv.   .)
There is no possibility of not having
to stand there, for it says in another
place, " we *must* all appear" before it.
(2 Cor. v.   .) "When the Son of
Man shall come in His glory, and all
the holy angels with Him, then shall
He sit upon the throne of His glory."
(Matt. xxv.   .) And then He will
divide the sheep from the goats, and
He will make no mistake. And then,
surely and really, you and I will be

there, standing before Him where He puts us, on the right hand or the left, and none between. And then we shall be judged out of the things that are written in the books. (Rev. xxi.   .) And nothing can possibly be hidden or forgotten then, for God says He will bring every work into judgment, with every secret thing. (Eccles. xii.   .)

Oh how terrible, if we had never met our Judge before! No wonder that some will say to the rocks, "Fall on us!" (Rev. vi.   .) How shall we be able to stand in the judgment?

Stay, look at the Judge! Who is it? "Who is He that condemneth?" (that is the same word as "judgeth.")

Oh what a blessed answer! "It is Christ that died, yea rather, that is risen again, who is even at the right hand of God, who also maketh intercession for us." (Rom. viii.   .) Now do not you see how thankful and glad we should be that *Christ* is our Judge, Christ Jesus who came *first* to save us !

But even this would not be enough to give us confidence at His coming. (1 John ii.   .) For He is "the righteous Judge" (2 Tim. iv.   ), and "will not at all acquit the wicked." (Nahum i.   .) A *righteous* judge cannot let people off merely because they know him, or even because he loves them. Ah! but see what the Love has done ! The Judge Himself has been judged in our stead, and has borne the punishment in our stead ! And His righteousness is reckoned to us. (Rom. iii.   .) Therefore we may say :

"Bold shall I stand in that great day,
For who aught to my charge shall lay?
Fully absolved through these I am,
From sin and fear, from guilt and shame."

Our Hope.

"Jesus Christ, which is our Hope."—
1 Tim. i.

THERE are two very different ways of using the word " hope." One is when we say " I *hope* so," with such a tone as to show that we don't very much expect so! Now if you look out all the texts about it, you will find that God never uses it that way. In His word hope always means bright, happy, confident expectation. So that must be the sort of hope He means us to have.   He says " Happy is he . . . whose hope is in the Lord his God." (Ps. cxlvi.   .)

Sometimes if we ask persons whether they are " safe in the arms of Jesus," they look very distressed, and say, "I *hope* so," with a tone that says they are very doubtful about it. That is not a bit like the bright hope St. Paul speaks of, when he says we are to "hold fast the confidence and *the rejoicing of the hope* firm unto the end." (Heb. iii.   .)

But we can only have a bright hope by having the right hope. There is only one true hope, and that is Jesus Christ Himself. If we are "without Christ," we really have "no hope." (Eph. ii.   .) But we need not pass another day, nor even another hour, without Him, in the dismal uncertainty of danger; you need not wait for anything at all, but at once flee for refuge to the Hope set before you, that is to Jesus Himself. (Heb. vi.   .) And that Hope will be to you "as an anchor of the soul, both sure and steadfast." Without it you are like a little ship driven about by the waves, and drifting every minute nearer to the rocks where she must be dashed to pieces. But with it you are like the little ship that is anchored safe on what the sailors call "good holding ground," and nothing can by any means hurt you (Luke x.   ), or take away your blessed hope. (Tit. ii.   .) For Christ Himself will dwell in your heart by faith (Eph. iii.   ); and He will be "in you, the Hope of glory" (Col. i.   ); and nothing shall separate you from His love. (Rom. viii.   .)

Happy, so happy ! Thy Saviour shall be
Ever more precious and present to thee,
Onward and upward along the right way
Lovingly leading thee day after day !

𝔥imself!

"Jesus Christ Himself."—EPH. ii.

YOU will say, "But this is not a name of Christ at all." Perhaps not; and yet somehow it seems to me the sweetest name of any. It is what all the other names lead up to, the reality and the crown of them all. "Jesus *Himself!*" Do you know a sweeter word than that? I don't think I do! It seems to bring us right up to Him, quite close.

When the two disciples took that sorrowful walk to Emmaus, *Jesus Himself* drew near (Luke xxiv.   ); and there was no more sadness, but hearts burning within them, and the very mention of it warms our own hearts as we read. Then that same evening, when they were telling the disciples about it, "Jesus *Himself*" stood in the midst and said, "Peace be unto you!" (ver.   .)

It seems as if surely *any* heart must be touched, when we read again and again, "Christ also hath loved us and given *Himself* for us." (Eph. v.   .)

"Who gave *Himself* for us, that He might redeem us from all iniquity, and purify unto *Himself* a peculiar people." (Tit. ii.   .) "Who gave *Himself* for our sins" (Gal. i.   ), and, closer and more wonderful still, "gave *Himself* for *me*." (Gal. ii.   .) And then we read, "who *His own self* bare our sins in His own body on the tree." (1 Pet. ii.   .) Surely He meant us to be touched and softened and won by such a word!

Then we read that because we are flesh and blood He Himself likewise took part of the same. (Heb. ii.   .) So that " Himself took our infirmities, and bare our sicknesses " (Matt. viii.   ) ; (ought not that to comfort the sick ones?) and He *Himself* suffered being tempted, so that He might help us when we are tempted. (Heb. ii.   .) There are many other places that I might tell you of, but I would rather you would try to find the rest for yourselves.

Jesus *Himself!* He Himself loves you ; He Himself wants your love. It is all real and true; He Himself watches you as you read these words, and waits for your answer of love. Will not *you yourself* give yourself to Him now and for ever ? He is coming again ; and when He comes it will be Jesus Himself that you will see. " Whom I shall

see *for myself*, and not another." (Job
xix.   .)   No ! not another, not a
stranger (as you will see in the margin),
but "this same Jesus," "Jesus Himself." Then we shall know all the
sweetness and all the glory of the reality
of Jesus Christ !

> He Himself, and not another,
>   He who loves us to the end,
> King and Saviour, Lord and Brother,
>   Gracious Master, glorious Friend.
>
> He Himself, whose name and story
>   Make our hearts within us glow,
> He is coming in His glory !
>   Come, Lord Jesus, even so !

"Surely I come quickly."
            Amen.
"Even so, come, Lord Jesus."
                (Rev. xxii.   .)

Butler & Tanner, Frome and London.

Additional Names of Christ

NAME	SCRIPTURE
Our Surety	Hebrews 7:22
My King	Psalm 2:6; 5:2
_____	_____
_____	_____
_____	_____
_____	_____
_____	_____
_____	_____
_____	_____
_____	_____
_____	_____
_____	_____
_____	_____
_____	_____
_____	_____
_____	_____

OTHER RELATED TITLES FOR CHILDREN

In addition to *Morning Stars* we are delighted to offer several other titles from Solid Ground Christian Books for the young. Here is a sample:

Little Pillows and Morning Bells by Miss Havergal
The Child's Book on the Fall by Thomas H Gallaudet
The Child's Book on the Soul by T.H. Gallaudet
The Child's Book of Natural Theology by Gallaudet
The Child's Book on the Sabbath by Horace Hooker
Feed My Lambs by John Todd
Truth Made Simple by John Todd
The Tract Primer by the American Tract Society
The Child at Home by John S.C. Abbott
Early Piety Illustrated by Gorham Abbott
Repentance & Faith for the Young by Charles Walker
Jesus the Way by Edward Payson Hammond
The Pastor's Daughter by Louisa Payson Hopkins
Lectures on the Bible to the Young by John Eadie
The Scripture Guide by James W. Alexander
My Brother's Keeper by James W. Alexander
The Chief End of Man by John Hall
Old Paths for Little Feet by Carol Brandt
Small Talks on Big Questions by Selah Helms
Advice to a Young Christian by Jared Waterbury
Bible Promises by Richard Newton
Bible Warnings by Richard Newton
Bible Models by Richard Newton
Bible Animals by Richard Newton
Bible Jewels by Richard Newton
Heroes of the Early Church by Richard Newton
Heroes of the Reformation by Richard Newton
Safe Compass and How it Points by Richard Newton
The King's Highway by Richard Newton
The Life of Jesus Christ for the Young by Newton
Rays from the Sun of Righteousness by Newton

Call us Toll Free at **1-866-789-7423**
Visit us on-line at www.solid-ground-books.com

CPSIA information can be obtained at www.ICGtesting.com
Printed in the USA
LVOW08s2003010614

388126LV00001B/5/P